"Magdalena's poetry reflect
few people dare to take. Hei
despair of a 17-year marriag
shows it can be done with th
part of all of us: our intuition."
-*Sonia Choquette, New York Times bestselling author*

"This book of extraordinary poems describes the refreshingly
candid and raw journey of the awakening and self-liberation of a
modern-day female Rumi."
-*Jack Canfield, Coauthor of the Chicken Soup for the Soul® series*

"Magdalena masterfully articulates the poignant journey of a
woman's metamorphosis. Her words are a balm for the soul.
This collection is not just poetry; it is a celebration of self-love
and resilience, a testament to the glorious rebirth that rises from
the ashes of heartbreak and disillusion. A must-read for anyone
seeking solace and strength in their own transformation."
-*Sandy Hill, Author, Enthusiast, Adventurer, Athlete, Mountaineer*

"The transparency and vulnerability captured in Magdalena's
poetry speaks to the souls of all women. In a world where
women's voices are often silenced or whispered, Magdalena
boldly articulates our evolution and helps build our power."
-*Dr. Robin Buckley, Cognitive Behavioral Coach, TED Speaker*

"Magdalena's poems remind us of what a spiritual expansion all
relationships are, especially romantic relationships and the
relationship to self. A bold and beautiful book."
-*Kristin Hanggi, Director, Writer, Creative Guide*

"Such a beautiful, vulnerable and raw journey filled with
absolute love from the author to the reader!"
-*Taylor Simpson, Mentor to the Multifaceted Women of the World*

"Magdalena writes with fierce courage and unflinching
honesty. She shares her deeply personal story and journey of
discovery, self-acceptance, and ultimately the most beautiful of
all – self-love. Truly inspiring."
-*Michelle Nolden, Actor*

"Magdalena's poetry is like her spirit: powerful, unpretentious, inviting, and inspiring. Her contagious quest for expansion, full expression and finding real love is as authentic in her poetry as in her real life. Magdalena, thank you for being unapologetically you and making me look forward to being in my sexties!"
-*Bibi Brzozka, Teacher*

"Magdalena's poems have the power to give the readers wings and give their muted thoughts the gift of words. This book is not just an ordinary book, it's a freedom. It's a masterpiece and it's magical."
- *Uzma Ramzan, Spiritual Healer*

"An exquisite collection of poems that chronicles a woman's transformative experience pre- and post-divorce. The verses, profound and beautiful, explore self-discovery, break taboos around self-pleasure, and celebrate the triumph of rebirth. A positively empowering read."
-*Fanni Prokai, Founder, Mystra*

"Fortune favors the bold. And bold is written all over this book. Dear reader, you don't know what's coming yet but I can tell you that you are oh so lucky to have this book in your hands."
-*Jenny Quénard, Nature, Breathwork & Ice Bath Retreat Creator, Wim Hof Method*

"Magdalena's poetry forces us not just to look at the elephant in the room but to touch and caress it with compassion and self-honesty. Her evocative poetry offers us the courage to unapologetically embrace our true selves with vulnerability. Deaf hands waving."
-*Dawn Jani Birley, International-acclaimed Deaf Performing Artist; Founder, Creator & Artistic Director of 1s1 Theatre*

This book of poetry is an absolute TRIUMPH! It grabbed a hold of me from the preface alone and would not let go. Magdalena's poetry shares a universal energy of women everywhere; a rising from a shift from "going along to get along" to a new spirit of joy, aliveness, and honoring the wisdom within. Brava!
-*Cori McGraw, Founder, Love Academy for Women*

the day
i bought
a teddy bear
and
a vibrator

magdalena giovanna rosa

RED ELEPHANT PRESS

Run my dear,
From anything
That may not strengthen
Your precious budding wings.

— Hafiz

Dedication

To all love relationships
being conscious

But first,
I dedicate this book to the Divine Mother,
Prajñāpāramitā and Machig Labdrön

I dedicate this book to
my mother, Rosina,
and to the lineage of women before her.

I dedicate this book
to smashing the conditioning of living small,
subservient, not in one's personal power,
and not living out one's dream,
one's heart's desire,
in the one and only life we each are given.

I dedicate this book to my daughter, Dina
and our future lineage of women, should she choose—
May she go forward to live a life she loves,
living in her personal power and
living her heart's desire and dreams.

To all sisters,
to all women,

and yes, to all the conscious and loving men
who truly see and support us women.
And especially to the men who are not yet conscious;
they need this dedication the most.

And the final dedication:
To raise our children — girls and boys
(however that is defined) —
to be the best versions of themselves,
not at the expense of others,
but instead to align with
their own inner truth, wisdom and passion.

Preface

We women are a constellation of thrashing passion and caresses of tenderness.

Wanting the teddy bear is my wish for comfort and solace from hurt, despair, sadness, and what feels like things gone wrong. Really wrong.

The vibrator? Well. Ooh-la-la. Need I explain? Sensuality is not the same as sexuality, but most women have not escaped the conditioning of our patriarchal culture. (I envy you if you did.) So, the vibrator (yes, I will explain) is wanting self-discovery, of pleasure treasures in my body and beyond.

What you will find in these pages are seven years of my poetry as I write to untangle the mess of emotions I felt around my struggle to survive a seventeen-year marriage. I am Italian, female, and Catholic, which means I went to the ends of the earth to make my marriage work. But I was unhappy and couldn't understand why. And, of course, it was more than seven years, but it was then that I started writing as a way to listen to myself; as a way to heal myself, and by doing so became my own poetry shaman.

I wrote this book to wake myself up.
May it benefit all sentient beings.

This book speaks for the times in my life I didn't.

Table of Contents

Section One

Low Radiation

Low Radiation

I.

a single raindrop hitting a stone
on the same spot
warrants no attention

a few more drops
still nothing

but years later
decades later
you'll see a dent
or even a hole

I just couldn't ignore it anymore.

II.

a single raindrop hitting a stone
on the same spot

years later
decades later
you'll see a dent
or even a hole

unless you are a diamond.

Love Lights

You don't light up
when you see me.
I don't light up
when I see you.

Tiramisu

Like a piece of clothing
dropped from a thousand feet
I lay there
broken limbs
broken heart
eyes dull like charcoal.
Each inch of those thousand feet
tainted by cruel words,
being ignored,
not being seen or heard.

Feeling invisible
unheard
unseen
and mostly
deeply
unloved.

Who will save me?
Who will come to my rescue?

Long pause…
(like forty years)

I see a spark.
While it feels like ash and amber
I see a spark
deep within my heart.

Answer?
Me!

I will save me!

I am my last hope.

No one will save me but me.
Not my husband
        that's for sure.
Not my daughter
        it's not her job.
Not my friends
        they're too busy saving themselves.
Not my family
        same genes and issues?
But me!
Hlaksam NamDak
Yes, "personal responsibility"
as they say in Tibet.
If it's gonna be
it's up to me!

Bit by bit
doing what I love
doing what makes my heart sing

dancing
        signing
moving
        writing
all to save my life.

Tiramisu
"pull me up"
as they say in Italy.

Be real.
Be seen by me.
Be heard by me.

—

Be loved by me.

I see you.
I hear you.
I love you.

Everything But the Kitchen Sink

"How come this isn't in?" he mumbles as he places the plug back into the kitchen sink.

He has utterly ignored and overlooked the fact that she, his wife, his one and only, has thoroughly tidied up other parts of the kitchen for the last hour.

It wouldn't have bothered her so much if he'd sandwiched it with something
nice
kind
acknowledgements on both sides.

> But he doesn't.

Or
at other times, he might have noticed things worthy of complimenting.
like when she looked nicer than her normal average self.
Yes, he has said she is average looking.

> But he doesn't.

Or
if he focused on the good
40% of the time.
(51% would be ideal but hey, we gotta start raising the bar a little bit before it gets unrealistic)

> But he doesn't.

Or
flirt and tease

>But he doesn't.

Or
look into her eyes when he says thank you or gives her
things

>But he doesn't.

Repeat.
Repeat.
Repeat.

When did "I do" become "I don't"?

The Dam of Emotions

She asked him to dig up a couple of things: The How-To Manual she wrote and the 56 Reasons she loved him for his 56th birthday. She teased him that she needed to be reminded. And so, he took the time to not only dig them up, but he also found a plethora of other hidden treasures; a mountain of handmade and bought cards with her love-for-only-him poetry. It inspired him to reignite the ritual of card giving that they did so well in their earlier years.

A few days later, she found a card on her bedside table. She opened it. Nice. Touching words. But it didn't quite reach her... A part of her was long gone. Was it too late? Had all the years of noes, criticism and non-responsiveness to her requests killed off the love she had for him? The flame had dulled over time. It was the low radiation effect.

She wasn't sure how to feel. *Where have you been all this time?* a thought dared to whisper. *And now, all of a sudden, you expect me to be excited? And moved?* He had noticed no blip of excitement to his card but said nothing.

About a week later, they decided that they would reminisce together. Bad idea. Initially, taking each card was filled with excitement, like children taking their candy collected after a night of trick-or-treating; sorting out the goodies after a long, hard night of going out for Halloween in the neighbourhood. First, they reviewed the cards she gave him. She read and shared them with him. While he smiled and sometimes laughed, she, surprisingly, did not stir much. He quietly noticed.

And then they looked through his cards for her. He admitted, they faded by comparison. But that wasn't the issue. She knew words were not his thing, not his language of love.

A sense of dullness started to surface. She wondered: *had she become hard-hearted?* She questioned her ability to receive love. Why could she not feel any joy? Each card adding a bit more discomfort to the one before.
She couldn't understand it at first. Couldn't put words to it. It was like watching a romantic movie and knowing you weren't living like that in your own life.

Comparing? Then to now? Those cards captured a time of the erotic falling in love; the honeymoon phase, the drug of being in love. But there had been no sturdy bridge to the present. The mundane lifestyle of working, paying the bills, cooking and cleaning, did anything but that. They had become work mules with no fun. Well, actually, there was fun, but it was *his* fun; not hers. She couldn't understand her feelings… She just watched them. Observed them. Became curious about them. Honoured them.

And then, about an hour later, she burst into tears. The feelings started to have a name. Betrayal. Heartbreak. Disillusionment. Disappointment. Her tears continued to gush like an open dam of emotions no longer pent up. And then, for the very first time, she understood her own mother.

Her mother had told her the story about being greeted with the name of her hometown, "Faeto," instead of her own name, Rosina, after the longest journey ever: crossing the Atlantic. Her very being, discounted by words spoken. Unintentional, yet uttered. And done so by not just any insensitive man, but by her husband-to-be. How crushing that must have felt.

Hers were as intense, but not over a period of a ten-day ship sailing, but by a seventeen-year low radiation effect.

Careless Daggers

We harbour, and even fester,
emotions until they get some attention.
They hit a wound deep within us that we do
not even know exists until there is a trigger.
And
oh
the
triggers.

The painful trigger alerts us.
Our ancient voices say:
Heal me
I will continue to come until you heal me.
Pain
perpetuates
festers
repeats itself
like a broken record
layer upon layer.
We get crusty
lose faith in our dreams;
      in each other
            in our purpose and more.

And beneath the hurt
is a treasure

our Way of Being
buried
way

d
o
w
n

A Way of Being
          that moves the soul
                    to sway and swirl
— in a dance
          that stays fresh
                    and free.

But
we ruin it by
our unconscious reactions
and unkind words
throwing them at each other like

careless daggers.

My Truth

I feel like he lied
maybe it was me that lied

I am trying to sort it out

I want to see clearly
so that I know in my heart
my truth

Mask No Mask

the mask of having a husband
safe but
lonely

why am I so
afraid to take off my mask?

The Attack of Intimacy

they had a talk yesterday
and each time they do
it ends the very opposite of her intention

      she yearns
           to create
                      intimacy and connection

instead
what surfaces from deep within is
what appears to him an attack of criticism

he leaves the room
isolation replaces his warm body on the chair
she feels empty

My Grocery List

When my husband asks me to buy items at the grocery
store, I do.

If he says butter, bread, and a certain brand of coffee, that
is what I get.
No less.
No more.
Apparently, it is very important for a man that one does
this.

So, now, I ask for my grocery list.
"Hello Beautiful," was all I asked for.
A greeting in person,
on the phone,
or even as we wake up in bed together.

For years, it used to be "Hello Honey"
so, for me, this is an upgrade.
Something I want to step into.

It is a rather important and vulnerable request.
Hubby knows the reason.
He knows the story of when I was
a teen and told I was ugly.

So what happens?
Hello (25%)
Hi (25%)
Hello Honey (35%)
Hello Beautiful (10%)
Hello Gorgeous (5%)

—

Are you kidding me?
Two words.

Am I asking for too much?
I feel like a hypocrite here because a part of me sounds like a bitch.
The other part is struggling with my self-worth.

Damn.

The Poem is the Title 1

I have a security
blanket. But it
does not keep
me warm.

A Portrait of My Love Life

the vivid rainbow colours
splashed on the canvas
twirling swirling
dancing flirting
so much fun
pheromones dripping everywhere
gobs of passion
eyes locked
colours caressing
I love yous
flowers blooming
mountains moving

A lurking desert emerges in the background.
Speckles of carbon monoxide brown
Appear undetectable.

Criticism seeps into the foreground.
It starts to take over.
There is still time to save the masterpiece
But people are too busy.
Dark colours move in.
Gray and stormy clouds linger.
The bright colours are being threatened.
No one really notices
Or if they do, they say nothing
Or they say too much.
Nagging. Arguing.
More dark colours appear.
Some black. Stagnant. Sameness. Mundaneness.
Fun. What fun?

instead of a fresh canvas moving from left to right
where colours splash on
like someone reading
a long
long
beautiful
juicy sentence
now colours pile on top of each other
the love canvas has stopped moving

stagnant
caked on
brittle
like old dry paint on a wall
flakes fall off
from masterpiece to master mess

Marriage therapy.
Marriage courses.
Bright colours are added for a moment or two.
Light flickers on the canvas to re-discover the rainbow
colours.
There are some
But the damage has been done.
Deep into the core.
It would take a miracle to transform this painting.
The love is buried
If there is any love at all.

Some would say, just get a new canvas.
You mean a new relationship?
And others would say…
Work on it.
But the two people who created this mess-ter-piece
Are the artists who must ultimately decide.

—

One says work on it.
The other says "no."

Why does the one
who says "no" win?

How to Erode a Marriage

Complain
>and only focus on what your partner
>does wrong.

Overlook
>anything they do well.

Pass up on any opportunities
>to compliment them
>How they look, in particular.

Give each other
>looks of judgement.

Roll your eyes
>at their ideas.

And oh, yes,

Interrupt them,
>especially if they are speaking
>about something
>>important
>>>intimate
>>>>personal.

Take them
>for granted.

Treat them
>like they will allow you to mistreat them
>for the rest of their life.

And think that
>>they will actually stick around
>>so you can meet all your needs at their
>>expense.

Put down
>their ideas.

Only expect them to do what you want
and rarely
        if ever
do what they want.

And the real kicker?

Every once in a while,
do the very opposite
        of anything aforementioned
to give them
        a false sense of hope
that things
        might
                change
                        for the better.

Slow Torture

It is a slow torture
living here
in this home
with these people.

It is a slow torture
living here
in this mind
with these thoughts.

Outer becomes inner
inner becomes outer
what a vicious cycle.
Insane, in fact.

It seems
I cannot escape.
What is there left
to do
to be
to think?

Surrender.
Fully.
Melt.
Dissolve.
Let go.

Let God
hell, let Goddess
take over.
Be here
in the gift moment

—

yes, the present moment.

For here is the only place
to *hear*
what is truly happening.
The rest is a mental chatter of fog and suffering.

Stop saying *I hear you.*
Instead say *I here you.*

That is, be here and now
                    and be free.

The Poem is the Title 2

I can change daggers into
flowers now. You've
given me lots of
practice.

Thank you.

The Plastic Bag Trophy

After he ranted about
me leaving a to-be-recycled
plastic bag in a pit stop
before its actual destination

and him
having ignored how
tidy and clean the house looked

I decided to give him
The Plastic Bag Trophy
for mastering

the art of focusing
on the trivial
at the expense
of the essential

The Poem is the Title 3

I trust you with
my life but not
with my heart.

Cruelty

is taking the place
of the true lover
the sacred lover
who is meant to be with you
instead of
your current partner
who is loving you
half-assed
and out
of convenience

theirs or yours

Now
leave.

Free each other for that
true connection the soul yearns for —
with another
and to passionately dance together
with life and hold nothing back
not one iota

how dare you stay

Leave
now.

The Poem is the Title 4

For every day I stay
with you, I betray
myself.

The Dialogue about Loneliness

I am so lonely, she said.
I am so lonely, he said.

Can we be lonely together?
they asked each other.

If we do that, then maybe we won't be lonely.

After All These Years

he bought her
lingerie
simply
because she asked

was that all it took?

Section Two

Teeter-Totter

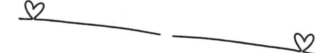

Teeter-Totter

Oh! I want to be sexy but to who?
To my husband?
To myself!

He just wants to talk money and numbers.
36-24-36

There's too much hurt between us.
I'm hurting for him.

Impossible.
I'm possible!

He just wants to talk kitchen renos.
He is so practical.

He is planting seeds for our future together.
Our future or his?

Let's play now?
He keeps saying no.

Teeter
Totter

Do I Stay or Do I Go?

There were still many good things.
We were making some inroads.
We were doing our "state of the union"
check ins
daily
weekly
and almost monthly.

We still made love.

There was hope that we could not only
save the marriage
but make it even
better than before.

This is what I was going for.
And I was working my ass off
to make it happen.

Tenderness Was All It Took

Tenderness was all it took
to melt her heart
of leathering stone

There he lay warming her side of the bed
at first, she could not believe her senses
and then when she realized who was there
her heart melted a notch
or two or three

Kindness was all it took
to remove a brick off The Great Wall of China
one by one
removing the barrier
dissolving her wall of pain

It was as if her heart was behind The Great Wall of China
protecting herself from more pain
from her own husband

Kindness was all it took
to remove a brick here and a brick there
from The Great Wall of China

Or shall I say The Great Wall of Vagina

Also known as
The Fox

Please tame me she whispers
You have not yet tamed me
Tame me
So in time you can take me

and let me be wild
thrashing with passion and love making

But until then
be patient my prince
Tame me with your tenderness
your kindness
your gentleness

It is the only way to melt my heart
The heart of my soul
as well as the
heart of my orgasm
inner orgasm

For I am like a wounded animal
perhaps because in eons past I have wounded
but now I am the one
wounded

Caress my soul-sores with love
Lovingly embrace my pain with compassion

And then she began to softly moan
Dim lights caressed her eyes
while his lips
yes, his lips caressed her skin
her lips
her shoulders
her neck
her breasts
her nipples
oh — her nipples
she moaned a bit more

—

they seemed to dance a sweet dance
like young hearts getting to know each other
for the first time perhaps
even though their bodies were a bit
wrinkled here and there

You see, their bed has been a desert lately
mundane, stress making a mess
inside and out

so this night was like sweet grass in the sunset
unexpected
and all because
there he lay warming her side of the bed

Tenderness was all it took.

You Just Know

How do you know?

When I was single…

How do you know he's the one?
I would ask married women.
They would say
You just know.

After seventeen years of marriage…

How do you know when to leave?
I would ask separated/divorced women.
They would say
You just know.

You just
no

Love Spoon

I opened your Christmas gift

it was a love spoon
you carved out of
our old kitchen cupboards

I melted

you really do love me
I thought

more moments like this
and I would surely stay

the scale tips this way

why are these moments
so far and few in between

the scale tips that way

and it really is a charming
love spoon

the scale tips this way

What I Want — Part 1

I don't want a divorce.

I just want you to
stop putting me down
stop dismissing me
stop criticizing me.

Discarded

Sometimes I feel like
a used piece of clothing.
You got what you needed

had your way with me
and tossed me to the wayside.
Sure, you say, we had wonderful times

together, but they don't seem so wonderful
when they're not for growing old together
to reminisce about.

Disrobed

disrobed
slowly undressing
kimono off the shoulder

tender kisses on the neck
robe falls to the floor
with pleasure

Languages of Love

Funny how a clean house is
foreplay for my husband.
When he walks into our home
there is an instant frown of disapproval
if things are all awry and scattered about the house.

But oh
how his eyes twinkle with delight
when things are all in order as he opens the door.

And well, for me
I long await the words to fall out of his mouth that say:
"My, you look lovely this evening."
or
The playful and flirtatious
"Ooh-la-la! I can't wait to…"

      I will leave that to your imagination
      and
      Oh, I hope you have a wild imagination.

But once we can figure out
and know the other's
language of love
it is a completely different world.
And in different ways, we each are saying
The same thing:
You are my one and only.

Now that calls for
A clean and tidy Ooh-la-la!

Two Scenarios of a Many-Year Marriage

It was not because they were bad people.

In fact, both were lovely and kind persons.

It was because they did not love themselves first.

So, they each did some work on themselves. They learned
at last to love themselves first. Initially, it was painful.
Very painful. Digging deep within themselves to discard
the conditioned beliefs handed down to them unconsciously
for generations. Their hands got dirty. Very dirty.
Sometimes, it felt like they were cleaning off oil crud. They
scrubbed and scrubbed. They cried a lot. They let go. And
they learned healthy ways to love themselves first.

And after learning and practicing all kinds of tools (like
Two-Chair, Feed Your Demon Meditation, Death
Awareness Meditation, Ho'oponopono, Tonglen
Meditation), they each looked into the mirror and were
moved to tears. For the first time ever they each loved who
they saw. Within themselves, they discovered that they
were their own best friend.

And now
when they looked at each other
in-two their eyes...

Scenario One

They wondered how on earth
they had gotten together.
Their interests were so different,
As were their values and
What brought each of them joy.

They saw deeper than with their eyes;
They saw with their hearts.
They realized that beneath all
Their disappointments with each other
They no longer blamed their partner.
They forgave themselves.
And they saw their own Truth.
What resurfaced was
their genuine love for each other
which had been drowning
beneath expectations and egos.
What they truly valued was the same.
What brought them joy was the same.

They laughed and cried.
They celebrated.
They hugged.

And they agreed to free the other
from this unconsciously
mismatched bond that had occurred like
two chemical ions
floating in a toxic world.

And they agreed from
this day forward to honour Self

---

before the other
so that they would only feed
their love for each other.
And this knowing
set them free
to be themselves
in each other's company.

And each went their own way.

They looked in-two each other's eyes
and said, *I see you.*
And they lived a very loving,
conscious, and extraordinary
life together.

feeling so grateful for the experience
for it was the long years together
that finally woke them up.

In the Kitchen

We were both standing in the kitchen.

"The only reason I am staying is because I am afraid to leave."

I said it
first.

And then
he said it.

Perhaps this was the only thing we agreed upon.

And then I looked up and said:
"This is not a good enough reason to stay."

I want more than this.

For staying feels like a mediocre poison.

Beach Entry

I gently step into the water
toes only
oh, toes only…

> as he gently kisses my bare shoulder
> my body melts and whispers *more, please*
> the thin strap of my white camisole slides
> down my arm
> with the help of his warm hand

the warm water greets my toes
and invites my feet to enter
one at a time

> my anticipation builds as his warm lips
> explore my body
> in seemingly new ways; like the first time
> sweet and tender
> caressing me lovingly

I feel the water splash my shins and knees
oh, my knees
the water teases my legs with such a refreshing touch
I sense an awakening

> our lips finally meet and I'm all in
> there is no room in my mind for the usual
> distracting thoughts
> two bodies talking as if for the first time
> like new lovers

the water reaches my thighs

        oh, my thighs
        his tongue has arrived between my thighs

lapping waters
        lapping tongue

smooth and cool
        building heat and excitement

I surrender and allow the water to wet my skin

        take me
        just take me

water to navel
        lips to navel

water to breasts

        oh, my breasts
        nipples celebrate with ecstatic joy

I am completely immersed in the water
swimming free
naked

        his man-ness swirling with my woman-ness
        inside outside
        pleasure climbing
        no attachment but simply present

a merging: water and body
a merging: man and woman
senses present
sensually present

     and even as I write this, I re-live this moment
       excitement runs through my body
         even the unspoken parts

thank you to the water for such a sweet encounter

It is Time

To do that which you fear the most.

Feel
and feel deeply.

One way or the other
you choose:
Fall in love with me with unbridled expression
or leave me.

Both will set you free —
on all levels.

Either way
a part of us dies and becomes anew.

When we choose to let go of who we think we are
and step into who we came here to be.

Trauma Bond

this marriage
is toxic
too good to leave
too bad to stay
indecision
slimy and irresponsible
but she is blind to this
due to her own
sense of being undeserving

it's no one's fault
We all succumb to
something mediocre
safe and secure
comfortable and numbing

it started
innocently
unbeknownst to her
and it started young
its weeds creeping into her soul
quietly
unnoticed
no scent or smell
rather invisible
but deadly
oh, so deadly
it kills passion and dreams and hopes and joys
it smashes confidence and self-assuredness
and clarity of the mind
deafened to inner wisdom
and is like
a carbon monoxide of the soul

—

unnecessary noes
fear stuck like barnacles inside the heart
ignorance of our own innate magnificence
and others
if the truth be told
we think small
of ourselves and others

and the young girl grows up into a woman
unaware of her beauty
inside and out
believing and gorging
on the stingy faded compliments of wounded people
for she is so hungry to be seen
truly seen
heard
truly heard
which are the very things that nourish a human being
a human soul

and then she fumbles and bumbles onward and outward
settling for breadcrumbs instead of a feast
and marries
and gives birth
and the cycle repeats itself
like a disease
a virus
an infection

how does one stop this painful and vicious loop
and get off the hairy-go-round
of unconscious living
or shall I say dying?

thaw
melt
that numbness and the numbing-out state
it takes courage
sheer bravery and gut-wrenching truth
the kind that no longer sells one soul for
the "please-like-me" from another

no longer the ice-cube

she begins to melt
revealing the hidden wiggling worms
of incredible discomfort-able emotions
and disturbing thoughts
rejection
feeling invisible
love me only when I am good and smart
sexual assault
crossing boundaries that should have never been crossed
betrayal of others
betrayal of the self — unknowingly

forty — maybe even fifty years later
she awakens
she now has the tools to melt and be ready
to embrace that which was frozen from fear
and pain

the journey begins
she begins to feel the deserving
she weeps
painfully and joyfully — almost in the same breath
for she has started
by severing the trauma bond

—

and by doing so
she sets them all free
to become
and
to belong to themselves

the tethers are severed
and
fall to the ground
while the soul soars
to dance
unleashed and ecstatic
with life
to live
and
to be
truly and brilliantly alive

Love Bond

listening to my truth
deserving all that life has to offer
the passion, joy and laughter
the giggling and sparks of intimacy and love
the riches
inside and out

kind and loving

being with your true beloved
showing compassion in sickness or
just when we fuck up
and say sorry
as an act of love
purification and adoring
each breath together
until one day we die
in the arms of the other
knowing full well we truly deserved
and embraced the exquisite banquet this life has to offer

'cause we were kind and loving

Huggling

he asked to cuddle
I wanted to snuggle
we ended up huggling

Knowing the Difference

Badass women stay
in marriages worth fighting for

Badass women go
when marriages are not

Baby's Birth Story: His

It was the first time in seventeen years
That she asked her husband for his version
of their daughter's birth story
She was afraid he'd only tell her all the negative things
For that is what she has become accustomed to

And up until now — her asking —
He had never offered

He said:
It was beautiful

That seeing blood and body fluids
Did not bother him

That once he saw their daughter's head and shoulders
emerge
It all happened so fast

That the midwife allowed him to do everything
Catching their baby

Placing their newborn daughter on her belly
Watching her crawl to her breast
And feed

And that the midwife
Clamped tight the umbilical cord
Before cutting it

And that if she had asked before
he'd have remembered more details

She thinks and hopes that every mother
Asks the father of their child for his story
To get their "eyes" of such a miracle

Baby's Birth Story: Hers

she could feel the contractions
twenty minutes apart
starting at 4:00 am
today was the day!

hours later

their fresh newborn daughter crawled up her mama's belly
she really did
her journey was not long
one, possibly two movements
instinctively, she latched onto a nipple
to receive her first taste of life, nourishment, and love

their bodies will always remember that moment

in that moment
she was complete
she was in awe and amazement
blessed beyond words
filled with an overflowing love
for their new family

who is this little being?
who will she become?

The Million Dollar Baby

At birth, each of us is worth at least
a million dollars.
We are priceless, in fact.
As time goes on, people hurt us and
we don't feel like a million dollars anymore.
We even sometimes
get into debt.
Or we sell out
and rob ourselves of our treasured lives.

This million dollars is like our self-esteem.

And if I do it right, by the time I die
I will have made millions more
because I was kind
because I shared
and
because I loved others the
way *they* wanted to be loved.
So they knew, without a doubt,
they were indeed loved.

Hair

I have curly hair.
Lots of it.

It's been the bane of my life.
Most hairdressers, back in the day,
didn't know much about how to make curly hair look great.

Then I met Maya
and she did amazing things.

My husband liked my hair
Short
Straightened
Contained
No curls.

And me?
I like my hair
big
curly
wild and free.

How Do I Love Thee?
Let Me Count the Ways

Me sitting in his chair. He speaks:

I plant for you the pussy willow tree you wanted
      after I took out the cherry tree.
I plant for you a garden to feed you
      with tasty strawberries, blueberries and the like.
I make you breakfast each and every morning.
      I support you to do your solo retreats.
I fill up your car with fuel and check your oil.
      I attend your Gratitude dance parties online.
I buy you your favourite mint chocolate and black licorice.
      I find you a car when yours gets smashed,
after I come to "save you" that day.
      I give you a child.
I agree to marry you three times in one week
      in two different provinces
I do the dishes after you cook a meal.
      I give you massages.
I support your yoga business.
      I take you camping to lots of awesome places.

Endless nights I watch TV alone as you tend to your work,
endless hours.
      Why are you so busy?
            Haven't I done enough for you?

Me sitting in my chair. I reply:

You never spoke to my heart.
You never consoled my pain.
You never loved me for me.

Full Moon, Full Moan

her body just
         let go at
              last

it had been
       months
felt like years

tight
       uptight
stressed
       not mistress-ed
clothed
       not disrobed

but today
       something
           happened

     oh
        how did it happen
           and how can she
                make it happen
                    again

her body just
       let go
         and
           she soared

           swooning
      this way and that
           opening the doors

to her senses
to her heart
to receiving
to pleasure

hers
not his

as she floated
back down
she did not rush
she did not allow anything
or anyone to interfere

no request to reciprocate
none
she asked for what she needed
and it was to
just be
just gently
drift back

at her own pace
at last

The Toxic Dance 1

Two dead people
dancing a dead dance

Done

The Toxic Dance 2

And in the end
we are not good for each other

I thought our extreme weakness and needs
were the path to our personal transformation

But after all these years, the gap remains
and this hole in my heart pains

Perhaps, then, the transformation is in
the leaving

Breaking, Broken, Broke

You said I broke you
when I asked you to move out.

What do you think you were
doing all these years?

Section Three

My Beloved

The Day I Bought a Teddy Bear and a Vibrator

I.

I never really had a teddy bear as a kid.
At sixty-one, I was long overdue.
Very.

So, the day came when I bought a teddy bear.

To be honest, it was a sloth bear
as inspired by my good
friend.

We were talking on zoom.

She saw my anxiety climb higher
as I explained that today I would
have my first MRI.

They found something in my brain on a previous scan.

After her initial burst of
compassion, she said "wait"
and then disappeared.

I stared at the screen.

In her absence I wondered
with excited anticipation.

When she returned with
her plush toy
sloth family of three

I melted.

My inner child screamed
I want one now!
And so, my big self
took care of my little self.
I bought me one
the same day
on eBay.

II.

The sex shop
was jaw-droppingly intriguing
and very tasteful, I might add.
My sheltered life
had not exposed me to the adventures
of pleasure.
Even as a mature woman
though, I would have been
very open, curious, and willing.

What a selection!
So many options and choices
and sizes and colours
and ooh-la-la shapes —
as if I even knew the benefits of such things

How does one even choose a vibrator?
Let alone the *right* vibrator?

—

I suppose it would be a lot easier
than choosing a man.
On the shelf in front of me
I am looking at a fraction of a man
the part that a lot of men think represents
all of who they are.
After speaking with the storekeeper,
it was suggested I go measure myself.

WTF

Yes?... as I listened to her instructions
Yes?
Oh?!
Ummmmm...
Really?

You want me to...

When I was done, I walked out of that store
with the best fitting vibrator
a woman could ever dream of.

Falling in Love with Myself

At some point I realized it started with myself.
Like a seed.
I thought the answer was out there
somewhere.
The things that would make me happy.
The house.
The car.
The husband.
The baby.
The new job.
More money.

None of these external things worked
in the long run.

The happiness from these extrinsic
things was all short-lived and
didn't endure the test of time.

Eventually, I realized
   it
       was
             here
                   all
             along
        inside
myself

Priorities

no man
       is more important
                than my self-worth.

Me Talking to Me

You're not listening!
It's hurting so much.
Stop ignoring me.

her inner self said to her outer self

and so,
she stopped everything —
and listened

and then they fell in love

The Poetry Shaman Speaks

Write, my sweet.
Write.
Keep writing.

It will save your life
and you will live sweeter.

Write, my sweet.
Write.
Keep writing.

It will save your soul.
It will heal your heart.

And you will live your truth.

A Beautiful Thing

and one day
she decided she just couldn't do it anymore

live the lies
lie to herself
be miserable
feel unloved

so, she walked away

into a new world
where she lived her truth
        from her heart
she created her own happiness
        in her own way
she felt loved
        on her own account
and she danced
        so did her heart

it rippled outward
        and she attracted similar vibes
                and she found her tribe

it was a beautiful thing

A Portrait of my Self-Love Life

white fluffy mint puffs and pink baby elephants
sweet cotton candy and rainbow lollipops
hearts of all colours
cooing and wooing
love so, so sweet
tickling toes and giggles so heart-melting
to look at the baby girl
love is in the air
love is all around
breath-takingly sweet.

The love canvas is gentle and sweet
tender and loving.

Beige starts to creep in even before school starts
shadows darken the canvas
splotches of black, bruising blue and yellow
cruel words smear images into one another.

Colours start to smudge
rainbow lollipops tangle with puberty
hormones and being overly self-conscious
innocence and naivety plucked
like flowers off their stem by
sexual predators who get their way.

The canvas now caked with crusts of dried blood brown in place
of where pinks and mauves of laughter and wonder
should have been.

Blacks and browns of repressing deep
pain start to take over
for
decades.

And oh, for a moment or three
the rainbow lollipops appear once again on the canvas.

But these brushstrokes and paint
created by the subconscious
are not from the
here and now.

There is still time to save the painting.

A conscious canvas
the colours are vivid and luscious
full of peace and laughter
riches beyond compare
each brush stroke is a present
moment filled with divine self-love
it was always like that.

The real
journey of the heart has begun
and the true *master-peace* is emerging
and that is simply because
the painter is stirring from her deep slumber;
is waking up

with both eyes wide open
in this moment
I feel awake.

—

Adore Me

"Adore me, oh, please just adore me,"
She asked of her husband.

She was asking the wrong person.

Go to the mirror
And say:
"I adore you.
My One and Only Beloved."

And so, she did.
And that made all the difference.

Fall Madly in Love with Yourself

love yourself
the way you wish your beloved would love you
and that puts something in motion
beyond any understanding

run the bath water
add the rose petals

write the love letter
caress your smooth skin

look at yourself with adoring eyes of reverence
say I am the one
now and forever

buy flowers
shower yourself with the words
of love you long to hear

write poetry of the romantic kind
laugh and giggle

have naked picnics
on the bed

dance erotically to music
that moves not only your soul
but all the unspoken parts as well

fall in love with yourself
madly
you are your own Goddess
you are your own God

start to behave that way
and
perhaps you will
see your lover follow suit

for they will not know what is in the air
but they won't care
for they have been waiting and yearning
to love you this way all along

and oh
if you have not yet met your lover
your mate
and wish for one
they will all be running and
knocking at your door

and you will be able to choose
your one and only
your beloved

because you have first become
your own
beloved

The Hungry Ghost

Wanting too much
Always

Feeling satiated and satisfied
Never

Clutter
Hunger

Doing too much
Busy

Doing nothing, being still
Boring

When I
Take a closer look
This kind of busy is sort of a laziness
An avoidance
A numbing out

This so-called being nothing
is everything

I got it back-assward
Everything is too much, too busy
It is the opposite of what my
soul wants and needs
and it leaves me
emotionally starving
spiritually raped
and homeless of life's sensuality
and vitality of the present moment

as I frenetically go about my mindless busy-ness
like a chicken running around with its head cut off

Clutter is like a vomit of stench soul-abandonment
be it material things or an over-scheduled day planner

Where is the sacred space?

How can my sacred feminine breathe and live here?
in this utterly desperate chaos?
How can the locked tight seal of "too much" welcome her?

How can there be any room for just *being*?

Being
Love lives here
Love breathes here
The sweet scent of pure bliss
invites me to sink deeper into a
nothingness that sends me to the moon

The Presence of My Beloved

the newly blossomed pussy willows
greeted me this morning
as I stepped outside

my heart leaped with delight into
the presence of my beloved
in one form
awareness of the beyond

my hand reached up to caress them
one at a time
one by one
their softness sent me into an
oblivion of joy

Being Sixty-One

Sometimes
if I think too hard
I mostly feel
emotionally beaten up, criticized and unloved.

Which, of course, sucks.

This proves nothing.
This only proves how the ego twists everything.

Ego eyes
are critical and unloving.

So, if I smash the ego looking glass
Forever —

I am essence.
I am light.
I am love.

Say yes to love.

Give me the hammer.

Now.

Woman of Worth

It took me sixty-one years to find my worth.
and she was here inside of me
all along…

"Hi"
I said meekly
"I finally found you."

And she ROARED back asking
"What took you so long?"

And then she
hugged me passionately for the long separation.
and we became one
and dissolved into the universe.

Our True Nature

Do you remember
        when you were essence
                vast and compassionate

That squeezed
        inside the bottle
                of the body?

Do you remember
        when you
                were born?

Yes, you are
        the genie
                in the bottle

The vastness inside
        your human form
                at this moment

Do you remember
        not being inside
                the bottle?

You must remember when

Through Loving Eyes

If someone was always watching you
how would you be?
Would you be any different?

Would you be kinder to others?
Would you be kinder to yourself?

Would you still stuff your face behind closed doors?
Would you still yell at your child?
Your husband?
Your wife?

Would you still grab that cell phone while driving
to text someone
en route?

Would the abuse stop?
If someone was watching you?

Well,
I have something to tell you.

There is someone watching you.

No,
not God
not anything outside of you.

The someone who is watching you...
is...

You
Your truth

Your inner voice
Your karma cam
Your mind stream
Your inner child

You.

So, the practice is this:

Start watching yourself
with the most loving eyes possible.
Shower yourself with these loving eyes
Such that your actions inspire these loving eyes
to love you even more.

The watcher
the watched
become one.
The gap disappears
and you are set free from any discrepancies
whether someone is watching you or not.

Until then
You are not free
I am not free
and this we know.

Let's
be free
loving eyes to loving eyes
loving eyes from loving eyes
there is no difference.

Stretch of the Soul

You are drowning out the thoughts
that so need to be heard
Who?
You!

No
Me?
Ah… yes, me

I run away from them
Drowning out my thoughts
Drowning them out with distractions

Minecraft with a movie on the side
I'll have two orders of that, please
Social media gluttony
will surely make me psychologically fat
with the messy entangled thoughts
of Criminal Minds, killing zombies
and other psychotic impressions of what is out there
to become a part of me

Oh Goddess
Save me from myself
I don't know how!

A dog chasing its tail
or me running in circles
with one foot nailed to the ground
pivoting insanely
trying to escape

But instead
I drown
I go deeper into the hell of depression
into the depths of feeling useless
like a failure

Feeding the demon

Feeding the demon of self-hatred
The only thing that seems to be growing within

There is an antidote
a faint whisper, I hear
An antidote
What!?
Is there even an antidote
to this insanely depressing glob of tar
that sticks to my breath and very being
seemingly impossible to get rid of?

What is the antidote?
I am afraid I might not even want it...

Oh Goddess
save me from myself
for I don't know how

Another whisper
Dig deep within for the well
The well-th
The wealth

It was almost like an echo
The well, the well-th, the wealth
Dig deep

So deep
I no longer know where I am
or where I've been
That place
is the only place
that will fill the void...

And there is a helping hand
the hand of a Goddess
reach up
reach high

dig deep
reach high

hmmm
sounds like a stretch of the soul
the stretch of the soul
Didn't you know
everyone must go through this to reach bliss?

It's the ticket
the gateway

Be not afraid, then.
Dive in with unbridled passion
and unshakeable fear
and your courage will
shatter you into peaces
and then you can
reassemble yourself
into who you are meant to be in
this one and only precious life

And well-th
that, to me, is worth every ounce of
brutal anguish and gut-wrenching discomfort
of peeling off my skin layer by layer
into the bones and blood
of who I am now

Do it
Just do it
or I will just prolong the
brutal anguish and gut-wrenching discomfort
anyway

People do
survive the ring of fire
People do
rise above the tempering of the sword

And come out the other end
fearless
beautiful
wise
compassionate
enlightened

Becoming
my own heroine

Sitting with Depression

I sat across from her

you would save a lot of anguish, she said,
if you would just like yourself

My Beloved

in a dream
I met my beloved
and I discovered
in fact

she
was
me

Wise One

I love being with you
we have so much fun together
you take care of me
I take care of you

we revere each other
we adore each other
we bow at each other's feet

ah
and that's how
I've always dreamed it would be

and now
I will never settle for less

thank you
my beloved within

Conscious Love Making

I've tasted this kind of love making
      with my lover, my man

and when I did
      I went to heaven each time

then there is conscious love making
      with myself

self pleasure
      as a way to see the divine

now that is a completely
      different matter

Mic Drop

I once heard Mama Gena say

Self love is the best protection

Section Four

Without Influence

A Year After Separation

living apart from my husband
the father of our child

recalibrating who I am
who I want to be.
there is space to align with source
with my truth
without
the
influence
of someone else sharing
my breathing space.

incidentally
he found the same thing
was happening to him.

while this was gut-wrenchingly painful
and full of loss and grief
this was
the portal
to get me to
an
      inner
         freedom

        I had not felt in decades
           if ever

        and at a
          whole
            new
              level

Back to Square One

back to square one

separated one year ago
divorce upcoming

alone
seeking
sometimes wondering if
I will ever be in a relationship again

back to square one

stop
hold it right there

I've moved ahead
so far ahead of square one

I have
experience
backbone
boundaries
and
a broken heart

I am
wiser
stronger
more compassionate
and real than

ever before
I am not back to square one

I am an upgraded version of myself
because of what I have been through

like a Japanese broken vase
joined back together with gold
even more beautiful

Shattered

Being Italian, female, and Catholic
These are some beliefs I grew up with:

Men are always right.
even when they're not.

> SHATTERED!

>> Men can be both right and wrong.
>> Women can be both right and wrong.

Sex is bad and dirty.

> SHATTERED!

>> Sex is sacred and powerful
>> when practiced playfully, consciously, and
>> with consent.

Men are better than women.

> SHATTERED!

>> Women and men are equal
>> as we stand before
>> the Gods and Goddesses
>> within ourselves

> SHATTERED!
> DEAD!
> GONE!

Burned to ashes where they belong.
No longer destroying my joy and worth.

And from the ashes comes forth
the birth of a new me.

Watch
    Out
        World

Swamping

music
anger
rage
punching pillows
and swearing

music
grief
intense sadness
on the floor crying and melting
soaked in my tears

music
erotica
sensuality
feeling sexy
exuding my inner radiance

pivoting
deep emotions
blows my mind
and amazes me
and the women I swamp with

rupture to rapture

oh my goddess
we just do

My Noes and Yeses are Aligning

I used to say yes
when I really wanted to say no

~~NO~~ yes to having sex
~~NO~~ yes to buying something
~~NO~~ yes to giving too much to the wrong people
~~NO~~ yes to whatever so they would like me
~~NO~~ yes to just being nice

> Selling out
> Selling a part of me
> Losing a part of me
> Dismissing
> Devaluing
> Bit
> By
> Bit

I used to say no
when I wanted to say yes

~~YES~~ no to me
~~YES~~ no to a bath
~~YES~~ no to slowing down
~~YES~~ no to something I really wanted
~~YES~~ no to something fun

> Selling out
> Selling a part of me
> Losing a part of me
> Dismissing
> Devaluing
> Bit
> By

Bit

Did you know that
doing this can make you sick?

Now I say
Hell YES !
to all the right-for-me things

And
Hell NO !
to all the wrong-for-me things

And that is how
I left my seventeen-year marriage

And I now own all of me
I got me back

      bit
           by
                bit
                      by
                          bit

Too Much Not Enough

I gave you
      too much
            credit.

            I never gave
      myself
enough.

Reaching Out Reaching In

Sometimes I am scared to be alone.
What thoughts will come and fill the void?

After enduring the dark night of the soul last year,
I wonder if it'll come back again.

I wonder how I'll be able to handle it
without reaching out to someone.

Knowing damn well if it were to happen again
I'll have to reach *in* this time.

Will I be there for myself?
Do I even have a choice?

    There is a
            very
                quiet
                   soft
                      loving
                         voice

      whispering
              in
                  my
                     heart

Saying:

                    why
                         are
                             you

                         so
                    afraid
            to
        meet
me?

Pretty On the Outside

You are pretty on the outside
Very good looking, very handsome.

The real question is
Are you pretty on the inside?

All I Wanted

was to love
you but my mind
got in the way

Feels Like a
Shawshank Redemption Moment

It's a hard-to-watch film.
The only reason I do is for the exhilarating ending.

Sometimes I feel like I am going through the shit pipes
escaping to my freedom.

Where am I now?
I am coming out of those pipes
and it is starting to rain.

Glorious rain
pouring down on me
washing me of all my fears of being alone,
        my darkness, my pain
washing me of my depression
        and the lies of who I thought I was
washing me of a worthless existence.

I bask in this rain.
I am becoming me.

In anticipation,
I await my Morgan Freeman on the beach
with my box of hidden treasures.

But now I am not in such a hurry.
I am savouring the journey
each step of the way.

And I know it keeps getting better and better
because I am learning to live in each present moment.

There is no better.
Better is now.

Becoming of Age

Didn't happen at 16.
It happened at 61.

My Own Blanket

I wrap myself in a blanket of soft sadness

    family broken

        heart broken

            dreams broken

a thin layer giving me warmth

but this time

    this is my own blanket

        gentle

            listening

                kind

I will sit here tenderly

until

    sadness

        melts

            away

Outer and Inner

I ask him:

How could you
lie to yourself
for so long
and drag me
with you?

My inner beloved asks me:

How could you
lie to yourself
for so long
and drag me
with you?

Let's Talk About Sex

we just gotta talk about it
                    sex
            love making
                        pleasure
            self pleasure

putting a taboo on sex
            just makes something so natural and beautiful
become tainted, twisted and warped

            how can something so magical
            that creates family
be so forbidden?

An Uncomfortable Question

Can a husband
rape his wife
by accident?

If she doesn't say anything
like "no"or
"not now"
and stays silent?

And her body
doesn't respond to his advances
or writhe with any sign of pleasure

and he enters anyway?

Before you spiral down and feel sick
and you should feel sick
this is oh-so-common.

Unintended hurt but
unconscious selfish sex
          on his part
passive non-consenting submission
          on her part.

Women don't speak up.
          Men don't clue in.
She didn't.
          He didn't.

We've all been conditioned
Women feel taken.
Men feel entitled.

Yoni Speaks

You have shitty boundaries

Too soon
Too many
Too fast

How can I pleasure you
*   when you don't value me?*
How can I take you to the moon
*   when you don't ask permission*
*   and ring my temple bell?*
How can I show you the universe
*   when you repeatedly give your power away?*

How long will it take before you
*   see me*
*   love me*
*   revere me?*

Only then
*   will I share with you all the secrets of*
*   love magic*
*   and true bliss*

For I am the sacred portal
*   to all of this*
*   and more*

If...

a man
asks a woman

if they can have sex
and she says no

and he then
pouts

please, woman
run the hell

away from
him as fast

as you can
and don't

ever go
back

Why Didn't Anyone Ever Tell Me?

The day I discovered that I, and
not my husband, was
responsible for my own
sexual pleasure and orgasms

I literally dropped to the floor and
bawled
my eyes
out until they were bone dry.

Why didn't anyone ever tell me?
Why did I give away all that juicy power
to a man?

No more.

Now I can transform
my story
not only in the bedroom
but outside the bedroom
too.

And I am.

Goodbye Vibrator! Hello Wand!

I only used the vibrator a couple of times

        I found
              something
                    better

                    The wand.

Goodbye vibrator!
            Hello wand!

               The wand

                      sleek
                              smooth
                                    obsidian
                                            crystal

I am in charge

        I know
              where to lead her

        I know
              the pressure
                    the rhythm

she
        heals
              me

she
    helps
        me

climb
    my
      ladder
         to
           bliss

I Danced

my way through the
first year of my separation

I burlesqued
I pole danced
to save myself
to keep my soul
intact

who knew
fun would be
such great therapy?

Happily Married

I thought if anyone could beat the odds, we could
After all, we had a communication like no other

      — wait… did we?

But people fall from high places
      they do
      we did
What happened?

I mean I loved you with all my heart
I adored you
Did you adore me?

And as I continue to move through the messy middle
hoping soon it will be the messy end
there have been
bouts of exhilarating freedom
      Lots
bouts of fully-expressed joy
      Lots
bouts of dark loneliness
      Lots

But at least
I am starting to be me
again
I am starting to see that
I am happily —
separated
And you know where that leads…

happily married
to myself

I am Sexty-One

I feel sexier and more beautiful than
when I was in my marriage

I am happier and freer
I even feel richer

I would have thought that being
with a man I'd feel all these things

Ah… being with the
right-for-me man, perhaps

After separation I was set free
but first I had to go through that threshold

of the dark night of the soul
sometimes I was afraid to go to sleep

this journey is not for
the faint of heart

it is for those
who want to rise above

the lies of what society says
we should want in our lives

Unapologetically Me

I wear an invisible cloak
made of iron chains.
I'm sorry
linked to
another
I'm sorry

that
goes
on
forever.

It does not belong to me
nor my mother's
but I wear it anyway.

The chains have burned
into my flesh.
We have become one.
I walk heavily upon this earth
weighted down.
Saying I'm sorry.
Breathing out I'm sorry.
Breathing in I'm sorry.
Living a life of I'm sorry.
A hundred times
A thousand times
A million times

For what
Am I sorry for?

For being a woman?

———

For being excited about my life?
For being bold and creative
      and different?
For being trusting and honest?
For having a sparkle in my eye;
      a joie de vivre?
For allowing the divine
      to live through me?
For feeling sexy and alive
      and sensual?
            — even at my age?
            — or shall I say,
                  especially at my age?

These are no-things
      to be sorry for.
These are beautiful attributes
      that guide me
            to live a full life
                  with no regrets.

This is my uniqueness;
      my essence.

These iron chains;
a cloak I now see.
      I rip off me
            with wild abandonment
I no longer allow
      myself to burn a slow death
A silent suicide
      of endless I'm sorrys

I am free to be me
naked from others' expectations

melting the conditioning
I am no longer afraid
   to speak my truth,
      to ask for what I need
         to ask for what I want

I can dance alone
   on the street
      I can feel free
         with sensual pleasures
         I can walk away
            from toxic people

I can let it all go
   and start anew
      I can now delight
         in my own presence

I am not sorry
      I am soaring

I am
   unapologetically me

Section Five

Revelations

The Poem is the Title 5

My intuition knew all along
I was just catching up

I Knew When...

I knew when...
>
> thirteen years ago
> you were coming back from a weekend
> with the boys.
> I saw you walk pass the kitchen window.
> Instead of feeling excited
> my body stiffened and contracted.
> I was bracing myself to be criticized.

I knew when...
>
> I saw a handmade artisan leather purse for $500.
> My eyes widened with a Hell Yes!
> and you said:
> "If you buy that purse, I will divorce you."

I knew when...
>
> your eyes didn't meet mine as you handed me my
> Valentine gift
> and you were already looking at our daughter
> to give her her Valentine gift.
> And
> it was the same gift.

I knew when...
>
> the day my mother died
> and we had important papers
> to sign the next day
> you said:
> "Why do we have to fly there right away?
> She's already dead."

I knew when…
        on New Year's Eve
        we were celebrating at home
        dancing and it was one
        of my favourite songs.
        You must have seen my delight
        but half way through the song
        you said:
        "This isn't my kind of music" and walked away
        off the dance floor.

I knew when…
        I knew
            but I didn't listen.

You bet I am listening now.

Damn, I wish I'd bought that purse.

Puzzle Pieces Becoming Puzzle Peaces

now I can put all the puzzle pieces together
those red flag moments
a long list

I denied what I saw
and definitely denied what I felt
instead, I stuffed them down to my toes

"shhh toes," a part of me said

looking back
they were trying to offer me
puzzle peaces

each one now
revealed and seen by my soul
like an archeologist digging for hidden treasures

it's safe now to come out and play
it's safe now to be me
I see all the puzzle peaces

and I am happy
from the inside
out

The Lingering Haze

"I believe I love you,"
the words fell
out of his mouth
mindlessly.

We are amicable
but every time we get
together something is left
behind when he leaves.

A lingering haze that feels
a bit like carbon monoxide.
Only a good love
detective could have picked
up on it much sooner.

It's been there for twenty-one years
but like a fish in toxic waters, she does
not know her surroundings until she
removes herself from them

and then
by sheer contrast
it becomes obvious to her.

My fish was not in healthy
waters. It was this lingering, hazy
something; a not such a good feeling
something; a slowly killing me
inside something.

Now I am out of this
something. Breathing in unconditional

self love and tenderness. Waking up to
my own beauty inside and
out. And oh, I do mean
inside and out.

Inside, heart, mind,
and sensual body. Yoni, rose petals,
dancing, body swooning, moving,
dressing my own unique way.

So, yeah, back to "I
believe I love you…"

We were discussing how I
want to be loved. Why was I telling him
anyway? Because it was my last ditch
attempt at saving our marriage —
a marriage not worth saving, I now see.

Fuck, how stubborn and
naively Catholic could I be?
Instead of seeing the writing
on the wall, I needed to hit my head
against the wall and come to my senses.

How do I want to be loved?
Let me tell you.

I want to be loved for me.
Nothing to prove.
Loved for me.
And, well, chased.
I like being chased.

And he said again:

___

"I believe I love you."
And in the same breath he said:
"I am not going to chase you."

So, this is what
unrequited love feels
like. No wonder my
fish was slowly dying.

I finally put a name to
the lingering haze.

DONE

I am worth way more than that.

I want to be loved for me.
Frolicking in the sea.
Romancing the stone.
Flirting with fun.

Giggling, touching, sensing,
honouring, loving,
and yes, having the
practical stuff, too.

I now know what I want.
And by knowing what I want
I also know how I
want to love another.

A Woman

I never felt like I was your woman
now I know why

I never was

The One

I so wanted you to be the one
but that wasn't possible
not because you were or weren't

it was because
I wasn't yet the one
for me

Filling Cups

It's not your job
to fill my cup

It's not my job
to fill your cup

It was wrong of me to think
you ever could

I must fill my cup
You must fill your cup

And then
we can meet
to do wondrous things
together

What I Want — Part 2

I didn't want a divorce.

I just wanted you to
stop putting me down
stop dismissing me
stop criticizing me.

Wait.
Holy shit…

You dismissed me
but I had dismissed myself first.

You were just
my mirror.

On the Right Track

I met a beautiful and grounded woman and I was
struck by her wisdom, confidence and presence

I asked her
how did you become so enlightened?

she looked me straight in the eyes
and gently replied
with one word

pain

Advice from My Dad

"Better to be happy alone
than miserable with
someone."

That was my dad telling
me when I was 16.
Now I am 61.

He only had a first-grade
education in Italy. Me? Too
much education.

Loneliness

I had an interview with Loneliness once.
    Many in fact.

The most amazing thing happened.
    And it was the sweetest miracle ever.

She wasn't lonely
    anymore.

Loneliness
    became Loveliness.

In the End (for Portia Nelson)

everything worked
out painfully perfect

loving you helped
me love me

thank you

in my next
love I'll take a
radically
different street

The Sacred Marriage

In the end, we are all wanting this:

the sacred marriage within
the inner queen marries her outer king
the outer king marries his inner queen

the feminine and the masculine
in balance and harmony
in one body

      mine

intuition with aligned action
living a magical dance
in one body

      mine

The king adores
and serves his queen
with ecstatic pleasure
in one body

      mine

The queen whispers
intuitively to her king
her powerful orders
from her heart

      mine

Only then can I step out into the world
to find union with another
and create the outer sacred marriage
with another being
two bodies

      ours

And oh, how sweet our babies will be!

What a delightful world this will be!

Hurt No More

You
      can't
            hurt
                  me
                            anymore
                    for I've
             stopped
      hurting
myself.

Paradox

We must know ourselves completely
before we entangle ourselves with another.

Yet, it is by being with another
that we get to know ourselves.

Intuition Peeks Her Head Out

is
   it
     safe
         to
           come
                 out
                    now?

PIE

I.

Pleasure
Is
Everything

II.

If you cannot allow
yourself to have pleasure
in the bedroom
how in heaven do you think it's gonna show up
anywhere else?

more PIE please

The Poem is the Title 6

I divorced
I partied

It Doesn't Get Any Better than This

I
    am
       so
          happy
to
    be
      with
        you

my
    inner
      beloved

a
 l
  l

    d
     a
      y

        l
       o
        n
         g

The Last to Find Out

will I ever be lonely again?
I am no longer running away from myself

she and I have met

I have found the hidden
treasure —

me

Maybe Just Maybe

I.

maybe just maybe
none of this happened

well, the victim ego stuff anyway
like a snake shedding its skin
the ego falls away
revealing the true self

a spiritual metamorphosis

II.

maybe just maybe
that's what this is all about

raindrops hitting a stone
but not just any stone
acknowledging the
diamond within

that was here all along

Woman

She embraces every part of herself:
    the goddess, healer, lover, alchemist, protector,
dancer, singer, poet, prophet, and creator,
    the sexy and sensual,
the courageous and vulnerable
    the wild and warrior
and so much more.
    She is woman.

The Last Poem (a Self-Portrait)

Acknowledgements

I have been a "workshop junkie" most of my adult life. I have spent thousands of dollars and hours cultivating the six inches between my ears, my "personal real estate," to be the best version of myself in this one and only life. (I've probably paid off the mortgage by now).

For the last few years, the following people have been my teachers, mentors, and role models. I owe them endless gratitude for their unflinching courage, extensive knowledge, and outstanding leadership.

Thank you to these leaders and teachers:

Bibi Brzozka
(Energetic Love Making)
You are a powerful woman who walks her talk and shows the world how much joy and pleasure there is "in the bedroom and beyond." Your programs are life changing from the inside out.

Briege Farrelly
(Medicine Woman)
Where it all started, my Heart Journey, and continues to this very day. Your work is filled with tenderness, compassion and magic.

Chris Duncan and Galit Reuben
(Conscious Education Company)
This is the first time I ever heard of that only 2% of

the world is doing "personal growth" differently. Absolutely magic. Chris, what a Superconscious and intuitive leader you are. Galit, you are an amazing coach with extraordinary talent and intuition.

Daniel Lobb
(Totally Responsible Person Enterprises)
Your coaching calls were powerful and insightful and helped me to take responsibility for my life.

David Karasek and William Whitecloud
(Create Your Destiny)
The mastery curriculum you offer takes living to another level. David, you are an incredible coach. William, your teachings are beyond extraordinary.

Julie Zivah
(MS, RDN, Parent Coach)
For seeing me for who I am and for coaching me to be the best mom I can be.

Kristin Hanggi
(Writing Coach)
You are the woman who makes dreams come true. What a model for living life to the fullest. Can I be you in my next life?

Lama Tsultrim Allione
(Feeding Your Demons®, Tara Mandala Buddhist Retreat Center)
Your teachings are beyond exquisite and transformational at the cellular level.
I am forever grateful.

Regena Thomashauer
(Mama Gena's School of Womanly Arts)
You are absolutely outrageous and showed me how
to "swamp'," "trinity," and "spring clean," which
were all medicine to my soul as I was navigating
through the first year of my separation.

Sharon Pope
(Marriage Coach)
Without your guidance, I would not be here.
Deep gratitude for your compassion, wisdom and
courage to be true to yourself.

Terri Cole
(Boundary Boss)
Your personal journey to be a Boundary Boss is
nothing less than inspiring, genius, and a model for
being my own personal leader and boundary boss.

References:

Kevin Lamoureux, PhD
The poet had an in-person conversation with Kevin
which clarified the many ways the word 'tribe' has
been used to wound and how it is used here with the
intention of healing. Used with permission.
Poem on p. 96

Kristin Hanggi
For her profound teachings at her retreat in Sedona
on Inner Queen and Outer King which inspired my
poem The Sacred Marriage on pg. 170

Maureen Murdock
For her important work, The Heroine's Journey
and inspiration for my poems, Woman on p. 180
and The Sacred Marriage on p. 170

Portia Nelson,
For her brilliant poem: My Autobiography in Five
Short Chapters poem on p. 169

Regena Thomashauser,
Founder of Mama Gena's School of Womanly Arts.
Swamping is a process she teaches. Poem on p. 126

Thank you to my fabulous writing and publishing team:

My editor, Wess Mongo Jolley.
So impeccable. So encouraging. Working with you
was magic.

My book doula, Caitlin Elizabeth.
So meticulous. So patient. Working with you was fun
and exciting.

Thank you to the following people for their support, unconditional love, and true friendship:

To my incredible yoga teachers for their ongoing
guidance and wisdom: Melanie (Madhuri) Phillips,
John Buchanan, Sherri Kajiwara, and Yvonne Jaques

To my "Dolphin Team:"
Arlene Ward, Renée Bueckert, & Lindsey Melnick
You are brilliant women and experts in your fields.

To Shayla:
My good friend and FYD partner whom inspired me to buy a teddy bear sloth in the first place and then for sending me a purple homemade sweater you knitted.

Thank you for the lovely artwork and bio photo:

To my daughter, Dina

To my proofreaders and proof listeners:

Antoinette, Barbara, Christine, Cori, Dawn, Dina, Gina, Fran, Georgia, Jenny, John, Julie, Kerry, Karen, Kim, Kirsten, Kristin, Laura, Lise, Lucia, Maria, Marilyn, Marina, Patricia, Renée B., Renée S., Robin, SharmaRay, Tarnjit, Trisha, Victoria, and Yvonne. Special attention goes to Dina, Jenny, John, Marina and Renee S. for your extra attention to detail. My heartfelt thank you.

To Maria Francesca:
My sister and dearest friend, whom was with me on the phone for hours during my dark night of the soul.

And finally:

To order a wand go to: MyMystra.com
A group of women from Mexico who are in the business of creating wands.

To save 10% use the code: PIE61
reminder: PIE stands for "pleasure is everything"

About the Author

Magdalena Giovanna Rosa is a poet, teacher, and speaker. This is her first poetry book. She is a loving mother to her daughter and currently lives in British Columbia, Canada. Find more at:
MagdalenaGiovannaRosa.com

Next Steps for Living Your 'Unapologetically You' Life

Once again, thanks so much for buying my poetry book: *The Day I Bought a Teddy Bear and a Vibrator: unapologetically me.*

How did you enjoy it? I love hearing from my readers. You can write me directly from my website: **magdalenagiovannarosa.com**

And while you're writing, tell me a little bit about yourself...

What made you buy my book? What makes your heart sing? And most importantly of all...

Did the book help you in some way? How will you use what you learned from the book in your personal life; in your self-love life and in other areas?

Also, if you liked the book, spread the word and share it with your friends. And please also review the book on Amazon and Goodreads.

This book is only the start of taking YOUR life to a whole new level...

Make sure you visit **magdalenagiovannarosa.com** for:

- How you can experience one of the most powerful personal transformational practices ever
- How you can become resilient after separation and/or divorce
- How you can book me as your keynote speaker for your upcoming conference or other events

I can't wait to work with you.